IMAGES
of America

CATALINA
ISLAND

Catalina Island is the enchanting Pacific isle just off the coast of Los Angeles in Southern California. Her history is rich, colorful, and intriguing. Through photographs of Catalina's past places, buildings, people, and events, the story unfolds of how visionary businessmen built the ultimate vacation destination. Join us as we explore Catalina Island's history.

IMAGES
of America

CATALINA
ISLAND

Jeannine L. Pedersen
Catalina Island Museum

ARCADIA
PUBLISHING

Published by Arcadia Publishing
Charleston, South Carolina

Library of Congress Catalog Card Number: 2004106994

For all general information contact Arcadia Publishing at:
Telephone 843-853-2070
Fax 843-853-0044
E-mail sales@arcadiapublishing.com
For customer service and orders:
Toll-Free 1-888-313-2665

Visit us on the Internet at www.arcadiapublishing.com

Water transportation played a large role in the development of Catalina Island. Early steamships made the island accessible and the ocean voyage more comfortable. The 25-mile trip took approximately four hours in the early ships. Many of the early steamers were beautifully appointed and by the 1920s, with advancements in steam engine technology, travel time to the island was only two hours.

CONTENTS

ACKNOWLEDGMENTS

This publication is dedicated to all past, current, and future donors of the Catalina Island Museum. All but four photographs in this book are part of the Catalina Island Museum's extensive photograph collection. Since the museum opened its doors in 1953, we have accepted more than 100,000 artifacts from hundreds of generous donors. It is the mission of the museum to collect, preserve, and share the rich history of Santa Catalina Island, and that is possible only through the generosity and foresight of our donors. Artifacts donated to the museum are used for exhibition, research, educational purposes, and publication. Through this publication, it is our goal to share with you some of the spectacular images that have been donated to the museum over the years and to thank every Catalina Island Museum member and donor for continued support. Enjoy!

INTRODUCTION

The photographs and ephemera pictured in this volume are all (excepting four) from the archives of the Catalina Island Museum. When we were approached by Arcadia about publishing a Catalina Island history for their *Images of America* series, we were certain we could easily fill a book with our photographs. And, in fact, what you see here is merely the cream of a very large crop. The museum, founded in 1953, houses a significant photograph and ephemera collection documenting the people, events, and "stuff" of our history. These materials primarily document a little more than 100 years of our history, conveniently the time period we wanted to cover.

Our curator of collections, Jeannine Pedersen, spent hours combing through our archives, selecting and describing the best images to tell the story of how Catalina Island came to be the world-renowned resort destination that it is today. That story began in 1887 when a department store owner from Michigan bought the island at the height of the real estate boom in Southern California. But the island's human history goes back much further than that.

People have been living on the rugged island for more than 7,000 years. Part of the chain of eight Channel Islands off the coast of central and southern California, Santa Catalina Island was first discovered by the European explorer Juan Rodriguez Cabrillo, claiming it for Spain in 1542 and naming the island San Salvador. Sixty years later, explorer Sebastian Viscaino reclaimed the island and gave it its current name in honor of St. Catherine's Feast Day. While these discoveries brought the island to the attention of the rest of the world, Native Americans had been making the island home for thousands of years.

Dubbed the Gabrielino once the Indians were removed to San Gabriel Mission and surrounding areas in Los Angeles, these people lived a life in balance with the island's natural rhythms. Gathering plants and sea life, they had an abundance of resources on the island that supported a population of about 1,500 people scattered throughout the coves, hills, and valleys of the island. Even so, trade with other islands and mainland tribes was important to their lifestyles. Sturdy wooden plank canoes plied the channel on a regular basis, carrying goods to and from the island. The island was a rich source of a soft, carveable stone called soapstone or steatite. Steatite was prized for utilitarian purposes such as bowls and ollas as well as decorative and ceremonial reasons. In later years, the Indians developed an elaborate and extensive trade network up and down the California coast with the coveted material. Catalina also became the center of a dynamic religious tradition that featured a powerful god named Chiningichinch. By the 1820s, the proud and independent island natives were removed to the mainland to be incorporated into the mission systems. Many lived in or near Mission San Gabriel, but it also appears that many worked on ranchos or moved further south.

In 1822, with Mexico revolting against Spanish domination, California and the Channel Islands came under Mexican rule. A little more than 20 years later in 1846, Gov. Pio Pico awarded Catalina Island in a land grant to its first private owner, Thomas Robbins.

The mid-1800s was an interesting time in the island's history. Ranching and mining were the predominant activities as early settlers explored ways to make a living on Catalina. While miners were caught up in gold rush fever, expectations had to be scaled back on the island. Gold was exchanged for silver, and silver on the island was found in a blend of minerals called galena. Silver was extracted from the ore, but it was costly, ultimately causing the demise of the mining industry on the island. Cattle and sheep ranching were successful for many years, but left their mark on the island. Even today, native grasses and plants are still crowded out by aggressive non-native species brought in during the ranching days.

During this time, ownership of the island passed through two other private owners—Jose Maria Covarrubias in 1850, followed by Albert Packard in 1853. In 1864, James Lick (of Lick Observatory fame) bought the island. The country was mired in the tragedy of the Civil War and even the island didn't escape its grasp, as it was taken over by the army in 1864, and a barracks and home were built at the isthmus. In claiming the island, the military removed most of the ranchers, miners, and squatters, leaving only a few well-established ranchers. The small army corps was on the island for less than a year as the army pondered the best use for the island. Military correspondence shows that they considered the island as a reservation for Native Americans from northern California, among other uses. But after nine months, they pulled out and left the island to an absentee owner who allowed the ranchers and speculators to move back in.

In 1887 the trajectory made a dramatic shift when developer and entrepreneur George Shatto purchased the island. I will leave the remainder of this story for Jeannine to tell through the wonderful photographs she chose to exemplify the changes the island went through over the next 100 years. These owners had the vision to see the potential of the island as world class tourist resort, while also building a close-knit community of residents. Each owner built on the foundation left by the previous ones, helping to create the island we all know and love today. This is the story of Catalina Island. It is, in the marketing words of William Wrigley Jr., "in all the world, no trip like this!" We think you will agree that in all the world there is no other story quite like this.

—Stacey Otte, Executive Director, Catalina Island Museum

One

DEVELOPMENT OF A RESORT COMMUNITY
GEORGE SHATTO

The development of Catalina Island as a vacation destination was first the vision of George Shatto, a businessman from Grand Rapids, Michigan. Shatto had real estate interests in Los Angeles and was given the opportunity to purchase Catalina Island in 1887. His intention was to develop the bay now known as Avalon into a pleasure resort and to lease other areas of the island to mining and ranching operations.

George Shatto's dream of a vacation destination soon became reality. He allocated thousands of dollars for surveys, plans, and maps of the island and quickly began construction of a hotel and

steamer wharf at the center of the bay. It was during this time that the city's streets were laid out, the city was named, and the first tourists began to travel to the island.

After the initial purchase of Catalina, George Shatto held a real state auction on the island. Once the town had been surveyed and streets had been established, Shatto decided to sell a number of lots to individuals and businesses. In July 1887, Shatto chartered two steamships to carry potential buyers to the island and the sale commenced once the passengers disembarked.

A real estate price listing from the "Town of Shatto" on Santa Catalina Island shows that dozens of lots were available for sale. George Shatto worked closely with Charles A. Sumner on the sale. Sumner was the real estate agent who brokered the original sale of the island to Shatto and is the namesake of Sumner Avenue.

Lots in the Town of Shatto

SANTA CATALINA ISLAND.

C. A. SUMNER & CO.. AGENTS,

54 N. MAIN ST., LOS ANGELES.

BLOCK 1.		BLOCK 4.—Continued.		BLOCK 15.	
LOT.	PRICE.	LOT.	PRICE.	LOT.	PRICE.
1 to 8	$1,000	18	$900	1 to 6	$1,000
9 & 30	1,200	19	1,000	7	500
11 to 13	1,300	20	900	8 to 10	400
14	1,400	21	900	11 to 17	150
15	1,800	22 to 32	850	18 to 32	500
16	800	33	800		
17 to 20	850			**BLOCK 16.**	
21 to 22	700	**BLOCK 5.**		1	$600
23	650	2 to 7	$1,500	2-3	550
24	600	8 to 16	300	4	500
29	550	17	1,500	5	450
26 to 30	600	18 to 23	1,300	6	425
31	700	24 to 30	1,200	7 to 24	400
32 to 35	300			25	425
36	200	**BLOCK 6.**		26	450
37 to 45	150	1 to 5	Reserved	27	500
		6	$600	28-29	550
BLOCK 2.		7	700	30	600
1	$1,800	8 to 12	1,000		
2 to 7	1,500	13	1,200	**BLOCK 17.**	
8	1,800	14	1,500	1	$600
9	800	15	1,000	2-3	550
10 to 15	850			4	500
16	825	**BLOCK 7.**		5	450
17	800	1	$1,000	6	425
18	775	2	900	7 to 24	400
19	750	3	700	25	425
20	725	4	600	26	450
21	700			27	500
22	675	**BLOCK 8.**		28-29	550
23-24	700	1	$950	30	600
25	675	2	700		
26	700	3	500	**BLOCK 18.**	
27	725	4	600	1	$450
28	750	5 to 13	1,000	2 to 14	400
29	775	14	400	15 to 27	300
30	800	15 to 20	350	28	350
31	825	21 to 24	300		
32 to 37	850	25	600	**BLOCK 19.**	
38	800			1 to 6	$200
		BLOCK 9.		7 to 9	250
BLOCK 3.		1 to 7	$200	10	400
1	$1,800			11	350
2 to 7	1,500	**BLOCK 10.**		12	350
8	1,800	1 to 5	$400	13	300
9	800			14 to 15	1,000
10 to 15	850	**BLOCK 11.**			
16	825	1 to 11	$300	**BLOCK 25.**	
17	800			1	$400
18	775	**BLOCK 12.**		2	500
19	750	1	$500	3-4	400
20	725	2	400	5	500
21	700	3 to 5	75	6	500
22	675	6	250	7	450
23	750	7 to 18	400	8	400
24	750			9	500
25	675	**BLOCK 13.**		10	300
26	700	1	$1,000	11	250
27	725	2	600	12	200
28	750	3 to 27	500		
29	775	28 to 31	50	**BLOCK 26.**	
30	800	32	600	1	$600
31	825	33	400	2 to 7	500
32 to 37	850	34	1,500	8 to 11	600
38	800	35 to 38	700	12	700
		39	600		
BLOCK 4.		40 to 48	500	**BLOCK 27.**	
1	$1,800	49	600	1 to 8	$500
2	1,500			9 to 20	300
3	1,500	**BLOCK 14.**			
4	1,500	1	$800	**BLOCK 28.**	
5	2,000	2	500	1	$500
6	800	3	400	2	350
7	850	4 to 12	300	3	300
8 to 15	800	13	1,000	4 to 6	350
16	900	14 to 22	300		
17	900			**BLOCK 29.**	
				1	$300
				3 to 7	250

The "Town of Shatto" was renamed by George Shatto's sister-in-law Etta Marilla Whitney, who believed the town should be given a name suitable for its beauty. She suggested "Avalon," a reference to Lord Alfred Tennyson's epic poem *Idylls of the King* and a word of Celtic origin meaning "Island of Apples." Tennyson's poem added another connotation to the word when he used it to describe a paradise of rest and contentment—the Celtic Isle in the western sea where King Arthur withdrew to heal himself of a grievous wound.

George Shatto built the steamer pier and the Hotel Metropole between 1887 and 1888. He purchased the SS *Ferndale* and began the first regularly scheduled steamship passenger service to the island. The ship traveled to the island once a day as it would take approximately four hours to cross the channel.

Avalon's first season as a resort community kicked off in the summer of 1888. The Hotel Metropole, located at the center of town on Crescent Avenue between Metropole Avenue and Whittley Avenue, played host to most of the visitors who ventured to the island that summer. It was the largest structure on the island and the center of activity.

If a visitor did not stay in the Hotel Metropole, it was possible to pitch a tent on the beach or in a designated lot. Escaping the hot mainland summers was popular during this time, and many resorts began to pop up along the California coast to serve those seeking a cooling breeze. Catalina Island was one such destination and renting a tent for a week, a month, or the entire summer was an affordable lodging alternative in Avalon.

One of the first private homes built on Catalina Island is known as the Holly Hill House, although its original owner named the house the Lookout Cottage. Peter Gano was a prominent Midwestern civil engineer who moved to Pasadena in 1880. Gano traveled to the island several times with friends and decided it was the perfect place for a home. Gano built the house with his horse Mercury between 1889 and 1890. He was a skilled woodworker and built a truly unique home. It remains one of Avalon's gems.

A long-standing attraction of the island has been its wide open spaces. During Shatto's ownership of the island much of it remained untouched. He leased areas to mining and ranching operations, but focused his efforts and money on the development of Avalon. Yet, the interior of the island was still explored by many adventurous travelers, and horseback riding and hunting excursions were offered to visitors.

By 1890, the small town of Avalon had grown from one hotel and a steamer pier to a burgeoning little resort community. Several homes had been built, businesses opened, and a new church was

under construction. The summer seasons brought many visitors and rows of tents appeared on the beach. Avalon was well on its way to becoming a premier resort destination.

Ranching on Catalina Island started in the mid-1800s. Many coves and beaches were used by ranchers that still bear their names, such as Ben Weston Beach, Gallagher's Cove, and Howland's Landing. Middle Ranch was established in the island's interior as a sheep shearing station. Many ranchers continued to operate on the island during Shatto's ownership.

George Shatto had an amazing vision for Catalina Island that he worked very hard to see become reality. He knew that the island had much potential and that his small resort community was just the beginning. Unfortunately, financial difficulties caused Shatto to default on his loans and he lost the island in 1891. Although Shatto's ownership of Catalina Island was short, his contributions have lasted for generations. Shatto is pictured here with his family and friends exploring the isthmus and Civil War barracks.

Two

THE OPPORTUNISTS
THE BANNING BROTHERS

Before their purchase in 1891, the Banning brothers of Wilmington, California were already involved with the island. William, Hancock, and Joseph Brent Banning were the sons of Phinneas Banning, a pioneer in transportation who was very influential in the development of Wilmington, California, and Los Angeles Harbor. The Banning brothers owned and operated the Wilmington Transportation Company and had provided much of the cross-channel transportation to the island for several years. (Courtesy of Banning Residence Museum Collection.)

When the Banning brothers heard George Shatto was losing the island, they saw an amazing opportunity. They had watched the island's popularity swell over the last several years as evidenced by increasing numbers of passengers on their ships. They decided to buy the island, and immediately began several construction and improvement projects.

The Banning brothers' first construction project was to build a dance pavilion. The round pavilion was built in 1892 to provide musical concerts and dancing for visitors. This was the first of many new attractions the Bannings had planned for Avalon.

Hancock Banning built a lovely home in Descanso Canyon in 1895. Originally there was no road that led to the home, and it was accessible only by boat. The Bannings later blasted a tunnel through Big Sugarloaf Rock for easier access to the home, but the tunnel soon collapsed. The home was later moved to make room for the new Hotel St. Catherine, their last construction project.

Joseph Brent Banning was a fan of the isthmus area of the island and decided to build a home there in 1909. He built his home in an ideal location as the sweeping view includes both Isthmus Cove and Catalina Harbor. Joseph Brent's home is now the Banning House Lodge, with 11 guest rooms, a great room with a fireplace, and amazing views of Two Harbors. (Courtesy of Banning Residence Museum Collection.)

Santa Catalina Island
Winter and Summer

Compliments
WILMINGTON TRANSPORTATION CO
Los Angeles Cal

HANCOCK BANNING
General Passenger Agent

F. H. LOWE
Asst Pass. Agt.

222 South Spring St.
AND
The Southern Pacific Co.
JNO. M. CRAWLEY,
Asst. Gen. Fgt. and Pass. Agt., 229 S. Spring St.,
LOS ANGELES, CAL.

The Banning brothers began to advertise the island as a winter and summer resort destination. They printed brochures that listed recreational activities such as fishing, hunting, bathing, boating, and stage coaching. Suggested winter activities include hiking, picking wildflowers, and enjoying the mild winter weather.

Under the Bannings, the picturesque town of Avalon grew into a bustling tourist destination. The brothers invested much time and money to ensure Catalina Island would be a resort that would lure visitors from all over the world.

The early steamships played an important role in the development and accessibility of Catalina Island. The SS *Warrior* and SS *Falcon* were two of the earliest ships that made regular trips to the island. The SS *Warrior* and SS *Falcon* were operated by the Banning brothers' Wilmington Transportation Company and were used as tugs in the off-season.

The SS *Hermosa* was launched in 1888 by the Wilmington Transportation Company and began making three trips weekly from San Pedro to Catalina Island in 1889. By 1893, the SS *Hermosa* made daily trips to the island during the summer as the number of passengers steadily increased. She was decommissioned from the fleet when the SS *Hermosa II* took her place in 1902. Her hull was later burned in Avalon Bay during a 4th of July celebration.

The SS *Hermosa II* was launched in 1902 and was a beautifully appointed addition to Wilmington Transportation Company's fleet. The ship drastically increased it passenger limit from 150 on the previous SS *Hermosa* to 700. As the island's popularity increased so did the size of the ships.

Greeting the steamships quickly became a daily tradition of Avalon residents. Steamer greeting activities began appearing on postcards as early as 1906. Diving for coins was a popular activity for the town's children. As the steamer would dock at the pier, children would row or swim out to the ship and yell up to the passengers "Throw a coin!"

The SS *Cabrillo* was launched in 1904 by the Wilmington Transportation Company. At the time she was the most luxurious ship on the Catalina run. She was equipped with a rosewood staircase, deep-pile carpeting, mahogany paneling, and a bar. The SS *Cabrillo* remained a favorite on the run for almost 50 years.

Wilmington Transportation Company's Banning Line to Catalina Island had a year-round daily run by the early 1900s. The company worked with the Pacific Electric Railway and coordinated the steamer departure with the Red Car schedule, all for a single fare. Passengers could take the railway from downtown Los Angeles to San Pedro and catch the steamer to the island.

Once the Banning brothers purchased the island they began to make immediate improvements to the amenities. By 1896 two additional wings and a tennis court were added to the Hotel Metropole. A ballroom annex, glass sun parlor, and cement sidewalks followed soon after.

The Hotel Metropole continued to grow throughout the Banning brother's ownership of the island. In 1902 a seawall was erected in front of the hotel where people loved to gather or swim. The Bannings also added "spoonholders" to the beach. These covered benches were a wonderful place to sit and enjoy the atmosphere—or romance a loved one.

As the island's popularity grew, so did the amount of tents. The rows of tents along the beach soon turned into "Tent Cities." Many lots were laid out along the city's streets to be used specifically for tents and each summer a city would be erected in canvas.

During the late 1890s approximately 80 to 100 tents would be rented each summer and this number grew steadily after the turn of the century. Renting a tent was the most economical accommodation on the island. For about $7.50 per week a tent could be rented that included beds, bedding, basic furnishings, and limited cooking facilities.

Families and friends often traveled together to enjoy tent life on the island. These groups made their escape from the hot mainland summer to enjoy the cool summer breezes.

Tent life on Catalina Island was filled with activity day and night. Days were busy with swimming, fishing, and exploring the island, while a lively game of cards was common among friends after dinner. These early visitors appear quite comfortable in their furnished tent residence.

The Glenmore Hotel was built on Sumner Avenue in 1891 by the same crew who built the Hotel del Coronado in San Diego, California. The Glenmore Hotel was the second hotel built to support the island's expanding visitation. There have been additions and remodels over the years, but it stands today as the oldest hotel on the island.

The island had many different lodging opportunities—something to fit everyone's pocketbook. The Avalon Inn was established in 1896 by Mrs. E. Allen. Located on Beacon Street, it was a popular accommodation for many years.

Beginning in the late 1880s, travel for pleasure and relaxation became highly popular. It was these adventurous Victorian-era travelers who flocked to Catalina Island during the summer season. It was quite fashionable to relax on the beach with your umbrella.

The beach in Avalon was the center of action during the 1890s. Many boatmen set up stands along the beach to offer visitors boating and fishing charters. Covered benches and glassbottom rowboats could also be found up and down the beach. Visitors enjoyed the adventurous atmosphere.

Swimming or bathing has long been a favorite pastime on Catalina Island. The bathing suit styles have certainly changed over the years, but the clear ocean waters of Catalina Island are just as inviting now as they were 100 years ago.

This view of the beach in the early 1900s shows a long row of benches for visitors to relax, as well as several beach side hotel accommodations, including the Grand View Hotel, Hotel Windsor, and the Pacific Hotel. On the far right is the Bath House built by the Banning brothers in the late 1890s.

The Bath House was equipped with changing rooms and access to the beach. It was a popular meeting spot and the best place on the beach to go for a swim.

The Bath House had a wooden staircase that descended into the water which presumably made getting in and out of the water in a wool bathing suit a bit easier. The Bath House also had a wooden float or raft for people to sit, stand, or play out of the water.

An interesting moment in Catalina Island history was the development of a carrier pigeon messenger service. The Banning brothers had been concerned about the island's communication link to the mainland, and the issue was solved by brothers Otto and Lorenzo Zahn of Los Angeles. They raised homing pigeons on Bunker Hill and started a winged mail service between Los Angeles and Avalon in 1894. The pigeon messenger service continued until 1902 when the Pacific Wireless Company set up a transmission station on the island.

As the island's visitation grew, so did the need for permanent residents. Many families wished to stay past the summer season, but their children would need to attend school. As a result, Avalon's first school was established in 1896. This private school initially held classes in a home on Metropole Avenue, but later moved to the Congregational Church where island students were educated for several years. This two-room public school was built on Whittley Avenue in 1901, with 59 students attending class during that first year.

By 1901, the Banning brothers had made several improvements to the island and its amenities. They built several new attractions for visitors and increased the amount and variety of tours. The island's visitation swelled each summer season as a direct result of the Banning's efforts and

advertisement of the island. Hundreds of tents popped up every summer, and new homes and hotels were built. This was a time of significant growth for the island—the time when many of the attractions and tours were established.

The aquarium was built in 1899 by the Banning brothers to offer visitors a glimpse of the underwater world. The aquarium contained 40–50 tanks of sea life. The attraction's amazing sea creatures fascinated many visitors.

The scenic Incline Railway was built by the Banning brothers in 1904. The United Engineering Company of San Francisco was contracted to survey and plan the railway. It started at the bottom of the town's south hillside, ascended to the top of the hill, and descended to the opposite side of the hill at Lovers Cove.

The Incline Railway stopped at the top of the hill where a tea room was built. Passengers could relax and enjoy the expansive view of Avalon and the ocean or take the railway down to Lovers Cove.

Upon arriving at Lovers Cove, visitors were offered a glassbottom boat ride. The marine gardens in Lovers Cove have always been a favorite spot to view the island's sea life. The railway continued service from 1904 to 1918.

Glassbottom boats are one of Catalina Island's earliest attractions. Documented as early as 1899, Catalina may have been the very first place to offer a glassbottom boat ride. (Florida might argue that fact!) The first glassbottom boats were rowboats with glass-paneled bottoms.

The glassbottom boat *Empress* was built in 1906 and was one of the first engine-powered glassbottom boats operated by the Banning brothers. A powerful underwater searchlight was added to the *Empress* in 1921.

The glassbottom boats traveled to the best spots on the island to observe the spectacular marine gardens. Moonstone Beach was a popular viewing area for the glassbottom boats. Passengers could also disembark and look for shells and moonstones on the beach.

The glassbottom boats were designed for optimal viewing of the island's marine gardens. Early passengers were amazed by the kelp forests and the abundance of fish in Catalina waters. They would also be entertained by glassbottom boat divers who would swim under the glass and point out interesting marine life.

Edgar Harrison was one of the famous professional glassbottom boat divers on Catalina Island. He would dive for abalone shells, sea urchins, and other marine life requested by enthusiastic observers. Edgar and a few other glassbottom boat divers could stay under water for a very long time. Harrison's record dive was 3 minutes and 51 seconds.

Arch Rock was a popular attraction for boat and fishing tours of the island. The rock was an impressive example of nature's work. However, its time as a tourist attraction was short, as the arch fell in the early 1900s.

The *Ning Po* was a mysterious Chinese pirate ship launched in the 1750s. The ship was used in Chinese waters for smuggling and piracy for many years. In her later years, the *Ning Po* was purchased by entrepreneurs and brought to America. In 1914, she was purchased by the Meteor Boat Company and brought to Avalon. The *Ning Po* moored in Lovers Cove during the 1914 season and served as a tourist attraction. In 1915, she sailed for San Diego and appeared in the Panama-California Exposition. She returned the next season and was moored in the waters of Catalina Harbor.

The Pilgrim Club was an exclusive men's gambling club built on Catalina Island in 1902. Operated by New York capitalists, the club was lavishly decorated with Turkish rugs, stuffed leather furniture, and works of art. A chandelier, which hung at the center of the great room, was rumored to have cost $300,000. Gambling stakes were high, and the club boasted that it operated as a miniature Monte Carlo.

Stage coaching was prominent on Catalina Island and offered as a tour for visitors. William Banning was an impressive stagecoach driver and would lead tours of the island's interior. The stage road was built between 1897 and 1898 under the direction of Samuel Farnsworth. Island residents were so excited about the road that they threw a party when the road from Avalon to Middle Ranch was complete.

One of the great stops along the stage road was Eagle's Nest Lodge, built between 1896 and 1898 by the Banning brothers as a hunting lodge and stagecoach stop. The construction materials for the lodge were shipped from the mainland and carried by mule to the building site. The lodge was originally constructed as a two-room wooden structure with a fireplace; a kitchen and shed were later added along with additional cabins that provided overnight accommodations for hunters and visitors.

In 1898 the stage road to Eagle's Nest was complete and the site served as a way station for the exciting stagecoach tours. During the stop at the lodge, the horses were changed and guests enjoyed lunch. Eagle's Nest Lodge also served as the headquarters for hunting on the island.

When the stage road to Little Harbor was complete, a small lodge was built at the site as a way station. The stagecoach tour would stop at Little Harbor so visitors could have lunch and enjoy the view. The Banning brothers set up a signaling system with the lodge. When the stagecoach driver reached a certain point, he would signal the lodge letting them know how many visitors he had on board so they could prepare lunch.

Catalina's first country club and golf course were built in 1892 just after the Banning brothers purchased the island. Initially a three-hole golf course was built, but it grew to a nine-hole course by 1894. The country club building was used as a clubhouse for golfers and had an adjacent tennis court.

The original nine-hole golf course had oil and sand greens due to the lack of water resources on the island, but that didn't stop golfers from playing this beautiful course in Avalon Canyon.

Catalina Island's Seal Rocks has been a popular attraction since the early 1900s. The Seal Rocks are located near the eastern end of the island, a short boat ride from Avalon. The Banning brothers offered boat tours to the rocks for visitors. The spot is still popular with seals and other marine life today.

Old Ben was a famous character in Avalon's early history. He was first noticed by sport fishermen who would throw their unwanted fish on the beach at the end of the day. Many seals and sea lions would swim to the beach to feast on the fishermen's leftovers. One sea lion, Big Ben, stood out from the crowd and quickly became a friend to the Avalon townspeople. He would pose for pictures and was always playful with swimmers. Ben was even featured in a Hollywood motion picture, *The Sea Nymphs*, in 1914. This postcard taken in 1915 of Bernice and Old Ben was sent all over the world by island visitors.

45

Musical concerts were an important part of Avalon's nightlife. In 1904, the Banning brothers built this large outdoor amphitheater. It was located on the south end of Avalon and could seat several hundred people. Band concerts were common on summer nights. On many occasions the band would play a concert at the amphitheater and then move down to the Pavilion for dancing. Visitors were often seen following the band from one concert to the other.

The Santa Catalina Island Marine Band was a staple of entertainment during the summer seasons for many years. They played at the Amphitheater and Pavilion to the delight of visitors for more than 30 years.

46

The first section of the Banning brothers wooden dance pavilion was built in 1891. The structure was used as a skating rink, dance pavilion, and auditorium. The Pavilion later became Sportland after the opening of the casino building in 1929. Sportland was an amusement center with archery, ping pong, snooker, and bowling. The building also housed Orton's Sandwich Shop during the 1930s.

The Catalina Island Marine Band poses for a quick photograph before they begin their daily concert on the Pavilion bandstand. The Marine Band was led by Charlie Porter and George Mulford.

Sugarloaf Point was Catalina Island's most recognizable landmark long before the casino building was built in its place. Sugarloaf Point was given its name by early sailors who thought the point resembled Mt. Sugarloaf in Brazil. Early visitors to the island would venture over to Sugarloaf Point for an exceptional view of Avalon.

During the 1890s, a vertical staircase was built on Little Sugarloaf Rock. The staircase led to a viewing platform where visitors could take in the beauty of Avalon. The staircase was quite dangerous; many of the adventurous travelers of the time would make it to the top, but then be afraid to descend. Local children would stand at the bottom of the stairs and offer to help people down for a fee.

Marine life has always been found in abundance off the shores of Catalina Island. When Avalon was first developed as a resort community, fishing became a favorite pastime of many visitors. The island attracted boatmen who offered fishing charters and most who visited tried their hand at fishing.

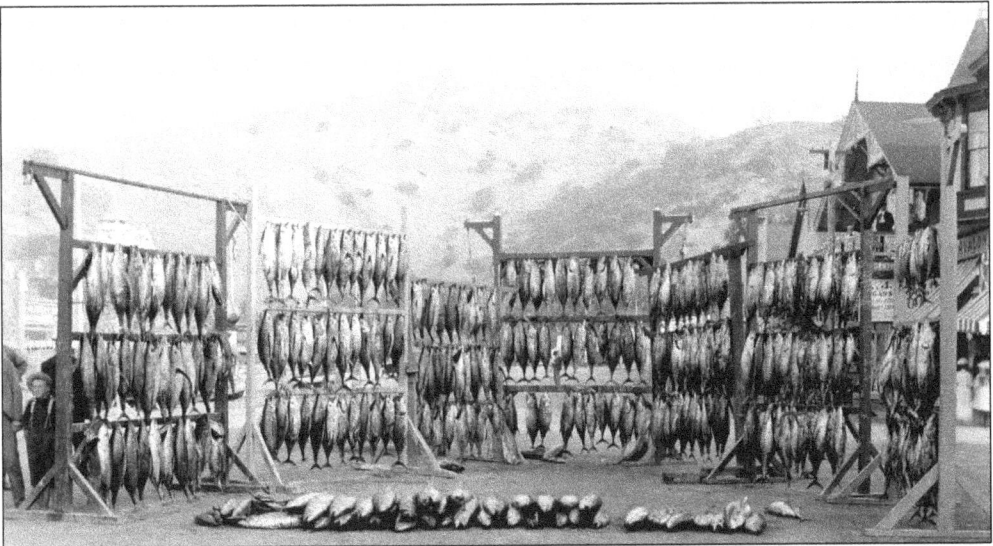

Many of the early fishermen used heavy lines and could catch many fish in a day. This albacore catch in 1902 shows how abundant marine life was on the island and how easily they were caught. This albacore catch took place in three hours with 20 fishermen and, unfortunately at the time, albacore was not considered edible so the fish were all thrown to the seals. It was such instances that prompted the formation of the Tuna Club.

The Tuna Club was established after the arrival of Charles Frederick Holder on Catalina Island in 1898. Holder was a respected angler from the East Coast and had traveled to the island to see if he could land a big fish in Catalina waters. He promoted conservation of marine life and introduced to the fishing community of Catalina the rod and reel, which gave fish a fighting chance, making it more of a sport.

When Charles Frederick Holder and his friends established the Tuna Club in 1898, they created strict angling rules and regulations. In 1908 they built a clubhouse, which today remains one of the most prestigious sportfishing clubs in the world. Many of its rules and regulations have been adopted by the United States Department of Fish and Game.

50

Charles Frederick Holder (left) with his historic 183-pound bluefin tuna caught by rod and reel in 1898. Holder later described his angling accomplishment as a 4 1/2-hour battle against a "leaping tuna" in Catalina waters.

Once the rod and reel was established on Catalina Island, fishing for sport flourished. Many boatmen opened for business offering charters to go out and catch elusive game fish. The island had many different species of large fish, including marlin.

Women were excellent anglers, and many were photographed with their catches. This 216-pound tuna was caught in 1903 with rod and reel.

Black sea bass are an immense fish that are found in Catalina waters. Many black sea bass were caught around the turn of the century until their populations began to decline. The black sea bass are now on the endangered species list, and only a few are spotted around the island each year.

This marlin was caught by L. Nixon on August 24, 1918, who was fishing with boatman Captain Halstead. The weighing scale on the Pleasure Pier has been the perfect photograph opportunity for hundreds of anglers. Everyone wanted to take home a photograph to prove their stories true. The boatmen also wanted to document their accomplishments to impress potential customers.

Charles Parker was a scientist who was originally sent to Catalina Island by the Smithsonian Institution in the 1890s to gather information and research island wildlife. One day a fisherman asked him if there was a way to mount his catch. Parker pondered this request and took the challenge. Charles Parker did mount that fish and many more after that. He found his trade and established a taxidermy shop on the island with his wife Emily, who took over the business when her husband died.

So many boatmen set up businesses on the beach that the Banning brothers feared the beach had become overcrowded. They wanted visitors to have more room to relax so they tried to remove the boatmen and their excursion stands from the beach.

The Banning brothers originally tried to build a pier parallel to the beach where the boatmen could land their boats and visitors could charter an excursion. However, the winter brought storms that quickly destroyed the parallel pier. The boatmen and property owners were dismayed by the Banning brothers' attempts to control them. In response, they established the Free Holders Improvement Association in 1909 to negotiate their interests.

The result of negotiations with the Banning brothers and the Freeholders Improvement Association was the construction of the Pleasure Pier, or known to many locals as the Green Pier. The pier, completed in 1909, provided a place for the independent boatmen and sightseeing excursions to set up stands and offer services to visitors. The Pleasure Pier is still used for these purposes today.

Charlie Paradise awaits his next customer at his stand on the Pleasure Pier. Charlie's display features photographs of his many catches, rods and reels and fishing lures—everything a potential customer needed to know about Charlie and his launch, Aubrey N. Paradise was just one of many fishermen who set up stands on the Pleasure Pier.

Glen L. Martin at Catalina Isl. in Hydro-aeroplane Looking for a Landing after Crossing Channel, May 10 1912

In May of 1912 an interesting event occurred in Catalina Island and aviation history. A young Glenn Martin flew a box-kite biplane from Newport Beach, California across the San Pedro Channel to Catalina Island. It was the longest over water flight and the first sea landing. A truly historic day!

Avalon residents were very excited to see Martin's plane over the bay. When he landed on the beach everyone rushed to see him and his interesting flying machine.

Avalon's location on the island lends itself to very gentle seas; its leeward position does not draw much surf. However, during the winter months, if the wind is blowing in a certain direction, Avalon can experience a northeaster storm. These storms have caused much damage over the years, but they are also very exciting to watch.

After 20 years of Banning ownership, Catalina Island blossomed into a wonderful resort destination with all of the amenities and attractions one could wish for. The Banning brothers invested much time and money into the development of the island, and they were finally starting to reap the rewards until one fateful night in November of 1915.

In the early morning hours of November 29, 1915 every citizen of Avalon was frightened from their slumber to the sounds of men running through the streets yelling, "Hotel's afire! Hotel's aburning down! . . . Avalon Town's aburning down!" Between 3:30 a.m. and 4 a.m. a large fire started near the Hotel Metropole. The fire quickly spread through town and by sunrise destroyed half of the town's buildings and homes.

In 1915 Avalon's fire fighting equipment consisted of a couple of hand-drawn hose carts and a volunteer fire department. The fire spread so quickly that the "fire department," which included every man in Avalon that night, could not keep up with the blaze. The ashes continued to smolder for several days and men patrolled the streets to ensure the fire would not start again.

The cause of the fire is still unclear; however, the November 30, 1915, issue of *The Catalina Islander* quoted Deputy District Attorney Keetch as saying, "It smacks strongly of arson," and he expected to make an arrest soon. According to an oral history interview with Hancock Banning Jr. taken in 1969, he also recalled that the fire was blamed on one man. According to Banning, "The story was that a man owned an apartment at the back of the Hotel Metropole and was about to be foreclosed, so he thought that he would get the insurance out of it and then a southeaster came up and burned virtually half the town."

Half of Avalon was destroyed in this historic fire. Six hotels were burned: the Metropole, Central, Bay View, Rose, Grand View, and Pacific, as well as the Pilgrim Club, Grill Cafe, Tuna Club, and the Bath House. Virtually every home between Whittley Avenue and Hill Street was destroyed, leaving many citizens homeless. The damage totaled more than $2 million, but the Bannings and residents of Avalon were determined to rebuild their town. The Bannings immediately began planning the construction of a new hotel to replace the large Hotel Metropole and several homes and hotels were rebuilt by the next summer season.

59

The Banning brothers made a valiant effort to recover their losses after the fire. They started planning the construction of the Hotel St. Catherine, which would replace the large Hotel Metropole. The original plan was to build the Hotel St. Catherine on Sugarloaf Point. The Banning brothers had Big Sugarloaf Rock blasted and leveled to begin construction of the hotel. A large hotel structure was planned on Sugarloaf Point and a hotel annex was planned for Descanso Canyon. However, their plans changed and ultimately the Hotel St. Catherine was built in Descanso Canyon.

The Hotel St. Catherine was a beautiful hotel and a wonderful addition to Catalina's resort atmosphere. The hotel included a large dining room, cocktail lounge, tennis courts, and a swimming pool. The Bannings built a wooden boardwalk that led from Avalon to the Hotel, which opened in 1918. Despite their best efforts to recover from the fire, the Bannings were still experiencing financial difficulties exacerbated by World War I and reduced tourism. The brothers began to accept offers from investors and eventually sold the island to a group of businessmen in 1919.

Three

A PLAYGROUND FOR THE RICH AND POOR
WILLIAM WRIGLEY JR.

One shareholder who purchased stock in the island sight unseen was William Wrigley Jr., of chewing gum fame. Wrigley, had a home in Pasadena where he retreated from the cold Chicago winters. There he met many Pasadena businessmen and entrepreneurs. Several of his friends were investing in the Santa Catalina Island Company, a company established by the Banning brothers in 1894. Wrigley's associates showed him a few postcards of the island to pique his interest and he decided to invest in Catalina Island.

Wrigley's curiosity was aroused and he decided to visit the island with his wife, Ada, and son Philip in 1919. He realized the island's potential and quickly decided he wanted to be the sole owner of Catalina Island. Wrigley bought out all other investors and took control of the Santa Catalina Island Company. Wrigley's vision for his island in the Pacific would bring many improvements to the island's infrastructure, build new attractions and steamships, and make Catalina Island known to the world!

Wrigley had many plans for the island and needed to set up residence on the island to see his plans come to fruition. He started construction of his home overlooking Avalon Bay in 1920. The building site was chosen by Wrigley for its amazing views and because the site received both the earliest morning and the latest evening sun. The home, built in a Georgian Colonial style, was finished in December of 1921 and included six bedrooms, a drawing room, billiard room, sun room, dining room, office, and terrace porch. Wrigley named his home Mt. Ada for his wife, Ada Foote Wrigley. The home is now a beautiful bed and breakfast inn.

One of the first attractions built by Wrigley was Sugarloaf Casino. Wrigley wanted to increase the island's musical offerings, and a bigger dance floor was needed. Wrigley built the Sugarloaf Casino on the spot cleared by the Bannings to build the Hotel St. Catherine. The casino had a bandstand and a large circular dance floor. The building also briefly served as Avalon's first high school.

Wrigley also built the Hotel Atwater. Opened in 1920, the hotel featured a large cafeteria that could serve 1,500. Said to be the largest in the world and covering an entire block, the cafeteria had two entrances—one on Metropole Avenue and the other on Sumner Avenue.

The Hotel St. Catherine was built just before Wrigley purchased the island. It was a beautiful hotel, and Wrigley maintained it as luxurious accommodations. So many celebrities loved to stay at the hotel that the gift shop proprietor wrote a weekly column for the local newspaper, *The Catalina Islander*, reporting star sightings. The Cocktail Corral lounge was a particular favorite among the stars.

The Hotel St. Catherine boasted the only swimming pool on the island for many years. The hotel's grounds also included tennis courts, private cottages and an incredible beach. The beach is still accessible to Island visitors; it is operated as the Descanso Beach Club.

Water transportation to Catalina Island has always been of crucial importance. Wrigley understood this and sought to increase the amenities and size of the Wilmington Transportation Company fleet. The first ship introduced by Wrigley was the SS *Avalon*. Originally built as the SS *Virginia*, the ship made the run between Chicago and Milwaukee on Lake Michigan between 1891 and 1918. She was requisitioned by the Navy, and Wrigley later tracked her down in a Boston Navy yard in 1919. The ship received extensive alterations and refitting in 1920 and carried passengers to Catalina Island for 31 years.

The SS *Catalina* was launched in San Pedro on May 3, 1924. Costing in excess of $1 million, the luxuriously appointed, 301-foot, three-deck ship carried more than 22 million passengers across the San Pedro Channel to Catalina Island in her 50 years of service. Both the SS *Catalina* and the SS *Avalon* took two hours, but the trip was filled with excitement. A band usually accompanied, and the ships had dance floors. Marine life was a common sight and couriers would roam the boat with information about the island.

Couriers were employed by the Santa Catalina Island Company to accompany passengers on the steamships and relay information about the island to those interested. A courier would give directions to your hotel, suggest an interesting tour, or take your picture. Essentially they were hospitality ambassadors for Catalina Island.

Steamer greetings were a standing tradition in Avalon by the 1920s and the Miss Catalina speedboats played an important role. Once the steamer reached the island, it would sail down the coast from Long Point and a "spieler" would give passengers island history and information. When the steamer approached the bay, the Miss Catalina speedboats would race out to greet the steamer. The speedboat company, founded by Al Bombard in 1921, offered visitors fast and fun rides for many years—with the steamer greeting the most popular ride each day.

Coin diving became a beloved tradition to Catalina Island. When the steamship would approach the pier, children would swim or row out to the ship and yell, "Throw a coin." The passengers would throw coins into the water and the children would dive to the bottom. The practice was quite lucrative for many island children.

On many occasions a band would greet the passengers as they disembarked the ship, often the big band in residence for the summer. Imagine stepping off the boat as the Jan Garber or Buddy Rogers Orchestra welcomed you to Avalon! Big bands were also known to serenade the departing steamer from the terrace balcony of the casino building.

Stevedores would greet the steamships at the pier and unload the luggage. At first luggage and freight were passed hand to hand, but a conveyor was later developed. The baggage and freight were put in carts, then rolled to the freight shed by tractors. Everything would be sorted in the freight shed and delivered to visitors, residents, and businesses.

During the summer season, it took a long time for the 1,000 passengers (on average) to disembark the steamships, which docked at the steamer pier located at the center of town. Passengers were led off the steamer pier, through the steamer landing, and into Avalon where they would be greeted by hundreds of residents and visitors.

The steamer greetings had grown to an elaborate affair by the 1930s. Hundreds of island residents and visitors would assemble at the steamer entrance upon the ship's arrival. All of the shops in town would close and people would come out of their businesses and homes. Over the years, personalities like Duke Fishman and Carl Bailey led people in singing and welcoming the island's visitors.

The steamer pier was the center of transportation activity for 79 years, growing over the years to accommodate the increasing numbers. Many passengers, much luggage, and tons of freight were loaded on and off the steamships over the years. This photograph shows the SS *Catalina* at dock along with the flying fish boat *Betty O*, and glassbottom boats *Empress*, *Princess*, and *Phoenix*.

Sailing across the San Pedro Channel in one of the steamships was not the only option for reaching the island. As early as 1919 the first regularly scheduled seaplane service was available. Syd Chaplin, half brother to Charlie Chaplin, began the first seaplane service between Wilmington, California, and Catalina Island with a Curtiss "Seagull" flying boat. Chaplin Airlines flew for only two seasons, but service was quickly picked up by Pacific Marine Airways.

Pacific Marine Airways, which began service to Catalina Island in 1922, operated three Curtiss HS-2L flying boats and a Loening Amphibian. Western Air Express purchased Pacific Marine Airways in 1928 and continued service to Catalina Island with a Sikorsky s-38 Amphibian, a Boeing 204 flying boat, and two Loening Amphibians until 1931.

The flying fish trip first began on Catalina Island in 1911. Capt. Joseph McAfee used to shine a light on the beaches at night as he sailed along the coast and noticed that California flying fish would leap out of the water in the light. He decided to mount a light on his boat, *Comet*, and take visitors out at night to enjoy the wonder of the flying fish. The *Betty O.* and the *Blanche W.*, pictured above, were both built by Wrigley as flying fish boats and named after his granddaughters Blanche Wrigley and Betty Offield.

Flying Fish, Avalon,
Catalina Island, Cal.

The California flying fish (*cypselurus californicus*) is the largest in the Exocoetidae family, a group of carnivorous or herbivorous fish of warmer seas. The fish do not actually fly, but glide on their outstretched fins for distances up to a quarter-mile. Their velocity builds as they approach the water's surface until they launch themselves into the air, vibrating their specially adapted tail fins in order to taxi along the surface. The fish uses this tactic to escape his impending predator. The light on the boat flashes on the water, simulating the silver streak of a large fish, thus prompting the fish to flight.

The glassbottom side-wheelers many remember, such as the *Emperor* pictured above, were built to accommodate the increased number of visitors who wanted to enjoy the island's incredible marine gardens.

The *Emperor, M.V. Princess,* and *M.V. Phoenix* were constructed with viewing wells that gave visitors a more comfortable way to enjoy the unique sea life. Today visitors are treated to prime underwater viewing on the island's popular semi-submersible tours.

Rowboat tug of war was a popular activity on the Fourth of July in Avalon. Five rowboats tied together would row backwards as hard as they could opposite another five rowboats. It was a real challenge, and many visitors lined the beach to watch the competition.

Stage coaching was the primary way to access the interior of the island during the Banning era, but Wrigley introduced the touring car. The touring cars were much more comfortable than the coaches, and drivers didn't have to worry about stopping to rest or change the horses.

The *Ning Po* was a Chinese pirate ship launched in the 1750s. It had a long life of smuggling and pirating in Chinese waters, but it would end its days as a tourist attraction on Catalina Island. The *Ning Po* had made a previous visit to Catalina in 1914 and spent a summer in Lovers Cove. After appearing in the Panama California Exposition in San Diego, she was brought back to the island and moored in Catalina Harbor.

The *Ning Po* was featured as a tourist attraction at Catalina's isthmus in Catalina Harbor for many years. The ship appeared as a backdrop in several motion pictures that were filmed in the harbor, but was later burned for one of those productions. As she was dismantled, chunks of her huge beams were saved by local residents who carved them into souvenir trunks and boxes. Fragments of this legendary ship still lie buried in the mud of Catalina Harbor.

Wrigley's most beloved attraction on Catalina Island was the Bird Park, built in 1929 and covering eight full acres in Avalon Canyon. More than 500 cages of varying sizes housed more than 8,000 different species of rare and exotic birds. Wrigley's private enterprise became one of the island's most popular attractions and boasted the world's largest aviary, several international award-winning birds, and free admission.

Catalina's Bird Park was one of Wrigley's dreams come true. He had long wanted to have an aviary where people could visit and study. The Bird Park had many different species including eagles, flamingos, mynahs, macaws, toucans, peacocks, ostrich, and penguins. The park was later scaled back during World War II when visitation to the island was limited. The park never regained its full glory after the war, and it was closed in 1966. The remaining 650 birds were transferred to the Los Angeles Zoo.

Ada Foote Wrigley (right) was the devoted wife of William Wrigley Jr. She enjoyed accompanying her husband to Catalina Island and made contributions of her own. Avalon's Chimes Tower was donated to the city by Mrs. Wrigley in 1925. She was also influential in the development of the Wrigley Botanical Gardens.

Avalon's Chimes Tower includes a $25,000 instrument manufactured by Deagan and Company in Chicago, Illinois. The instrument is designed to automatically strike on the hour, half hour, and quarter hour. The chimes can also be played manually at its electric console.

One exciting and little known fact about Catalina's history is that the Chicago Cubs held their spring training on the island for almost 30 years. Wrigley had purchased stock in the Chicago Cubs in 1916 and steadily increased his stake to later become the sole owner of the team in 1921. To be the owner of the Chicago Cubs was another dream come true for the dedicated baseball fan. Wrigley would travel to the island each spring with the team and rarely missed a game during the summer season.

Beginning in 1921, the Chicago Cubs traveled to Catalina Island for 2–7 weeks each spring for their annual training. The Cubs trained each morning and were encouraged to take full advantage of the golfing, fishing, hiking, and hunting. The team continued to train on Catalina Island until 1951, except during World War II when the Cub's trained in a barn in French Lick, Indiana. The team was happy to return to Catalina Island the following year. The Cubs considered Catalina Island their home away from home, and Avalon has long considered the Chicago Cubs its home team.

Wrigley decided a premier vacation destination had to have an 18-hole golf course, so he expanded the existing nine-hole course in 1929. He also built a new clubhouse that also served as the locker rooms for the Chicago Cubs during their stay. The beautiful new course attracted many golfers from around the world.

Catalina Island's golf course began to host tournaments that brought in some of the best professional players of the day. The Bobby Jones Golf Tournament was played on the island course for more than 20 years. This photograph shows Bobby Jones teeing off in 1931. The Catalina Open Golf Tournament was another match that attracted top professionals and hopeful amateurs throughout the years.

Wrigley had thought of many ways to advertise and promote Catalina Island, but none was more elaborate than the Wrigley Ocean Marathon. Wrigley promoted the island as a winter destination by having hundreds of people attempt to swim across the 22-mile channel in January 1927. He offered a $25,000 purse, winner take all! This lured more than 150 competitors to the island.

On January 15, 1927, the starter gun for the Wrigley Ocean Marathon fired. More than 100 swimmers jumped into the 58-degree water and began their brave attempts. Safety was a major concern of the competition; each swimmer had a rowboat, rower, and observer, and the boats were equipped with medical supplies, flares, and blankets. The SS Avalon was also converted into a hospital ship with doctors and Red Cross workers. After only six minutes into the race, the first swimmer was pulled from the water. By sunset, only 23 swimmers remained in the water. The race was finally won by Canadian George Young in 15 hours and 46 minutes. The marathon was a success and proved to be one of the most spectacular swimming races in history. It also brought attention to Catalina Island, Wrigley's ultimate intention. The risks of a winter swim outweighed the positives, however, and the race was never again attempted.

Wrigley did much to increase Catalina's attractions, steamships and national visibility, but he also made several less visible contributions to the island's infrastructure. One of his first moves upon purchasing Catalina Island was to recruit David M. Renton, a contractor from Pasadena. Wrigley convinced Renton to move to Catalina Island and take charge of the island's construction and improvement projects. Wrigley and Renton are pictured here at the Catalina Country Club, one of their many projects.

Thompson Dam and Reservoir were constructed in 1924 to create a fresh water system for Avalon. The reservoir collects water that is later pumped to a secondary reservoir at the summit and then down into Avalon. Thompson Reservoir was constructed to hold up to 200 million gallons of water.

When Wrigley purchased the island, communications were still dependent upon the wireless telegraph. Realizing the need for improvement, in 1923 Wrigley prompted the Pacific Telephone and Telegraph Company to install two submarine cables between Santa Catalina Island and the mainland for voice communication. The cables were laid on the ocean floor with the assistance of the U.S. Army ship *Dellwood*, pictured above.

The submarine cables are 23 miles long, each weighing more than 300 tons. The cables were the first American-built submarine cables and the first to be used exclusively for voice communications. In 1923, Pacific Telephone also built a central office in Avalon located at 135 Whittley Avenue. Manual switchboards were installed, creating many new jobs.

Catalina Clay Products got its start in the early 1920s when Wrigley and Renton were driving around the island discussing its potential. While backing up against a hillside in Avalon Canyon, near the current golf course area, the automobile became stuck in mud. Attempting to clear the mud from the tires, Renton discovered that the mud had clay-like qualities. Renton was intrigued and believed the clay might be useful for producing bricks. Wrigley agreed, and further research soon proved that the clay was perfect for bricks and other building materials. They decided to build a plant for clay production at Pebbly Beach, a rapidly growing industrial area on the island, just south of Avalon.

By 1927 the factory was in full-scale active production, which included three different types of face brick, hollow tiles, patio tiles and pavers, drainage tiles, and Mission-style roofing tiles. This line was integral to Wrigley's construction projects on the island. The materials were employed in the construction of the casino building, Catalina's Bird Park, and the country club, to name a few. In 1928 a decorative product line was introduced that included garden pots, vases, and tiles. The decorative line proved popular, and Wrigley hired skilled manufacturers and artisans to expand the line. By 1930 Catalina Clay Products launched tableware in three designs, as well as island souvenirs, a complete line of vases, candleholders, lamps, and novelty items.

The product lines developed by Catalina Clay Products were both beautiful and functional, and the advertisement and distribution of these lines brought a piece of Catalina Island into homes across America. Catalina brick and building materials continued to be an important part of the plant's success, but by the early 1930s, the art and dinnerware were outselling the original product line. Retail stores and displays were set up on the island in a number of places. This photograph shows the Catalina Pottery Shop built near the Via Casino entrance. A showroom was set up on the ground floor of the Casino and Catalina Pottery and Tile could be bought at the Bird Park and the Hotel St. Catherine.

Retail shops for Catalina Clay Products were set up on the mainland as well. The primary outlet was established on Olvera Street in Los Angeles. The line of decorative tile, art, and dinnerware known as Avalonware filled the shelves. Small shops, highlighting Avalonware, were also established in Wrigley's Arizona Biltmore Hotel and the Wrigley Building in Chicago. Avalonware could also be purchased in department stores across America. Catalina Clay Products continued manufacturing until 1937, when production costs increased and the venture was no longer profitable to the Santa Catalina Island Company. Several molds and the right to the Catalina name was sold to Gladding, McBean and Company, who continued to manufacture Catalina Pottery until 1942.

The Sugarloaf Casino, built by Wrigley in 1920, proved too small for the island's growing population. As a result, in 1928 the Sugarloaf Casino was torn down and the steel structure was moved to Avalon Canyon to be used as an aviary at the new bird park. The site was prepared and construction of Wrigley's new casino began. Architects Sumner A. Spaulding and William Webber designed the building at Wrigley's request with a ballroom over a movie theater in the Moorish Alhambra style with Art Deco fixtures, furnishings, and art work. The construction of the building lasted 14 months with crews working around the clock.

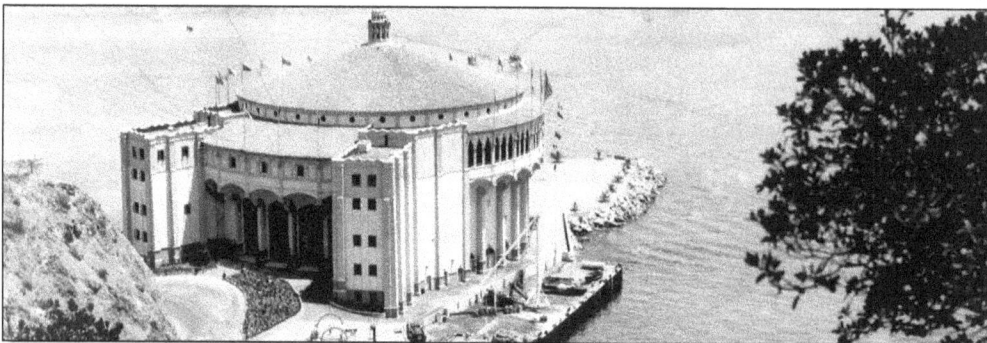

The casino building opened to much fanfare on May 29, 1929. Extensive opening ceremonies for the building lasted several days, and residents and visitors were in awe. The theater was originally built to accommodate 1,250 moviegoers and was one of the first theaters in America equipped for both silent and sound motion pictures. The ballroom was designed with a large circular dance floor that could accommodate 500 dancing couples. The Marine Bar soda fountain and a beautiful circular terrace surrounding the ballroom added the finishing touches. The word "casino" is an Italian word meaning gathering place or place of entertainment. The casino certainly lived up that meaning on its opening day and continues to be Avalon's palace of entertainment.

84

John Gabriel Beckman, a well-known artist best known for his work at the Grauman's Chinese Theater in Hollywood, was hired by Wrigley based on a design rendering submitted by Beckman with a distinctively Greek theme. His design later evolved to reflect the underwater surroundings of the island and regional historical and landscape motifs. Beckman and a team of artists worked day and night for three weeks to create the murals in time for the grand opening.

The casino ballroom was designed and built with a cantilever construction that made possible an expansive dance floor without supporting pillars. The dance floor was also carefully constructed of maple, white oak, and rosewood resting on a layer of felt and acoustical paper. The felt and paper are installed over a subfloor of pine that floats above support beams on strips of cork. Such careful attention was given to the dance floor to ensure a smooth and comfortable dancing experience. And dance they did! The ballroom played host to the most notable big bands of the day. Visitors had the opportunity to dance to the impressive sounds of Jan Garber, Kay Kyser, Bob Crosby, Buddy Rogers, Dick Jurgens, and Jimmy Grier, to name a few.

Via Casino Way originally had wooden arches that led visitors down the boardwalk to the casino building. When lit at night, the arches created a romantic ambiance that continued once you entered the building.

The casino building celebrated its 75th anniversary in 2004 with a tribute to the golden days of Hollywood and 75 years of music. Over those 75 years, the casino has been host to it all—motion picture premiers, the hottest big bands of the day, celebrities, USO shows, and much more.

"In All The World No Trip Like This" was one of the primary slogans Wrigley used to market Catalina Island to the world. And it was true! By 1929, Catalina Island had blossomed into a premiere resort community offering a range of amenities. There were accommodations and eateries to suit everyone's pocketbook, and the attractions and entertainment were first class. Wrigley's dream of a "playground for the rich and poor" had become reality. It was no wonder that Hollywood's elite flocked to the island for work and pleasure.

Catalina Island was quickly adopted by early Hollywood filmmakers and stars. The island has served as the backdrop for more than 200 motion pictures and has been transformed numerous times from an island in the Pacific to North Africa, Tahiti, and the American Western frontier to name a few. One Hollywood director who filmed at least three pictures on Catalina Island was Cecil B. DeMille, pictured here with his Marlin catch in 1919. He was quoted in *The Catalina Islander* as saying that Catalina is "the only place where I can get away to work amid real inspiration." DeMille was known for sailing to the island with screenwriters and his secretary in tow to work on a script over the weekend.

DeMille (center) is pictured here on the Catalina Island set of his film *Male and Female* in 1919. The film was a Famous Players–Lasky Film Production that starred Gloria Swanson and Thomas Meighan.

While Avalon and Little Harbor were used as locations for films, so many movies were filmed at the isthmus that it came to be known as the Isthmus Movie Colony. This photograph shows one of the many set buildings built by a motion picture company at the isthmus. Many of the sets are gone today, but one can still imagine tall ships at battle in Catalina Harbor during the filming of *Old Ironsides*, 1926, or the Tahitian village constructed on Isthmus Cove beach for the filming of *Mutiny on the Bounty*, 1935. In fact, many of the palm trees found at the isthmus today were originally planted as set decoration by the motion picture companies.

The most lasting contribution from Catalina's movie days was the introduction of the North American Bison to Catalina Island in 1924. According to *The Catalina Islander*, 14 buffalo were barged to the isthmus and released for the filming of *The Vanishing American*, adapted from Zane Grey's classic novel. Catalina Island eventually ended up on the cutting room floor of the movie, but the buffalo remained. The Catalina Island Conservancy now maintains a herd of 150 animals.

The city of Avalon and the island's steamships also played roles in motion pictures over the years. This photograph shows the cast of *Our Gang* aboard the SS *Catalina*. Through their filming projects, many actors and actresses were introduced to Catalina Island and fell in love. During the 1930s, celebrities were a common sight on the island.

Charlie Chaplin and his wife, Paulette Goddard, were frequent visitors to Catalina Island. Charlie and Paulette loved to sail to the island and try their luck angling for marlin and tuna.

Clark Gable spent much time on the island filming movies and relaxing. He was often spotted at the Hotel St. Catherine playing tennis or unwinding in the Cocktail Corral. Gable is pictured here at the isthmus signing autographs during the filming of *Mutiny on the Bounty* in 1935.

Mutiny on the Bounty starring Clark Gable, Franchot Tone, and Charles Laughton was one of the most successful movies ever filmed on Catalina Island, taking home the Best Picture Oscar that year. The movie was filmed primarily on the beach at the isthmus. A Tahitian village was built and many palm trees planted. Several ships were brought to the island for filming as well.

Zane Grey, famous author and world-class fisherman, first visited Catalina Island on his honeymoon in 1906. He was attracted to the challenge of deep-ocean fishing and had heard tales of the big game fish in Catalina waters. By 1914, Grey began to make annual trips to the island and later built a vacation home, the Zane Grey Pueblo, in 1925. He is pictured here with his unbelievable sunfish catch in 1926.

The Zane Grey Pueblo was designed to resemble a Hopi Indian dwelling and included 14 rooms, servant's quarters, and a work room. The home was finished with exterior stucco and rustic ladders leading to the roof. Grey spent many seasons on the island writing and fishing. His home is now operated as a hotel.

Winston Churchill made a quick visit to Catalina Island in 1929. He had heard much talk about the big game fish of Catalina and wanted to try his hand at catching a marlin. Churchill was quite fortunate and caught a 188-pound marlin in 20 minutes. Later in the day while enjoying a cigar at the Tuna Club, he reportedly wondered to club members what the fuss was all about. Most marlin catches can be quite a struggle, taking an angler up to four hours to land his or her fish.

Mr. and Mrs. Wrigley hosted several dignitaries on Catalina Island, including the Duke and Duchess of Windsor and former president Calvin Coolidge, who visited Catalina Island just after his presidential term had finished. Wrigley toured the president and his wife all over the island, including a stop at Catalina's Bird Park.

By the early 1930s, Catalina Island had become a thriving resort destination with a bright future. The island hosted thousands of visitors each summer season offering exceptional transportation,

accommodations, tours, and attractions. The best big bands delighted visitors in the casino ballroom and celebrities roamed the streets. Catalina Island was in the midst of its golden era.

TIME TABLE AND FARES

CATALINA ISLAND

IN ALL THE WORLD
NO TRIP LIKE THIS

April 1, 1933

Not only did Wrigley build upon the Banning brothers and George Shatto's efforts to create the resort community each owner had envisioned, but he also introduced Catalina Island to the world. Wrigley's advertising efforts and events launched Catalina into the consciousness of many Americans. Soon people were traveling from across the states and the world to experience the magic of Catalina Island. Wrigley established the foundation upon which the island still stands today. Unfortunately, Wrigley did not live long enough to fully enjoy his island paradise. He died in 1932, passing the reigns of Catalina Island and his international corporation, the William Wrigley Jr. Company, to his son, Philip K. Wrigley.

Four

FULFILLING THE DREAM
PHILIP K. WRIGLEY

After William Wrigley Jr.'s death in 1932, Wrigley's only son, Philip K. Wrigley, took over the Santa Catalina Island Company and ushered in a new era of development. Philip had been directly involved in his family's Catalina venture from the very beginning and had accompanied his parents on their first visit to the island in 1919. He had been instrumental in the development of several island industries. Although it was his father's vision that initially involved the family in the development of Catalina Island, Philip Wrigley's direct influence has also left a long-lasting impression.

Wrigley purchased a magnificent home on the island in 1927 known as Casa del Monte. The home is situated perfectly as it overlooks the entire city of Avalon and includes views of Avalon Canyon. The home was built in Spanish Colonial design with 17 rooms including seven baths, a breakfast room, reading room, reception hall, dining room, solarium, music room and a miniature theater. His descendants made extensive renovations in 2004.

Wrigley and his wife, Helen Atwater Wrigley, made many trips to the island each year during the winter and summer months. Philip is pictured here with close family friends outside of their beautiful Catalina home.

Wrigley took his father's dream for Catalina Island and went about fulfilling it. He took interest in the community and always had the island's best interests at heart. This photograph shows Wrigley with his daughters, Blanche and Dorothy, during a community parade in Avalon.

Philip and Helen Wrigley brought their family to Catalina Island often for visits. Their primary residence was in Chicago, but Catalina was their playground. This photograph shows Philip (right) with Helen, son William, and daughters Blanny and Deedie, enjoying a horseback ride through the island's interior.

Perhaps the most obvious impression left by Wrigley was the redesign of downtown Avalon. In 1934 Wrigley formally announced his plan to modernize the city of Avalon while retaining the charm and spirit of early California. Wrigley stated that, "We want to keep the best, not only in the City of Avalon, but in the modern conveniences that civilization has developed, and we also want to take from the past the things that are best, not only the architecture, but the method of living; the friendliness, the spirit and the utilization of leisure time, putting this in a natural setting."

Wrigley's plan included a complete renovation of Crescent Avenue, which had grown since the town of Avalon was founded in 1887 without any unifying plan. Crescent Avenue's new look would include two new fountains, brick and tile benches, planters with Catalina tile, grass walkways, palm and olive trees, and a serpentine wall. This photograph shows workers planting palm trees on Crescent Avenue in 1934.

This photograph shows the construction of the serpentine wall along Crescent Avenue. Wrigley's plan also included the construction and remodel of a number of buildings in the Spanish Colonial style, including the terminal building, steamer entrance, Casino archway, and the El Encanto. The early California feel was enhanced by Spanish-style uniforms for the bus drivers, couriers, and stevedores. Spanish troubadours met the steamers and strolled the streets of Avalon.

The El Encanto building was the showpiece of Wrigley's early California flare in Avalon. Opened in 1933, the El Encanto was the Santa Catalina Island Company's effort to preserve the traditions and culture of old California. The building and its activities radiated the spirit of early California, and with the assistance of the island's growing Mexican-American community, the El Encanto brought old California to life for thousands of visitors each season.

101

The El Encanto included a large open patio with Catalina tile tables and a central fountain. Many shops lined the patio featuring Mexican arts, crafts, and food. Many of the Mexican craftsmen were from Olvera Street in Los Angeles. Mariachis played and Spanish dancers would spin, to the delight of visitors.

Shortly after his father's death, Wrigley began the construction of the Wrigley memorial. The memorial constructed of concrete, local flagstone, and Catalina tile was finished in 1934. A few years later, Philip's mother prompted the planting of a garden at the base of the memorial. The Wrigley Memorial Foundation was later established in 1969 and the garden was enlarged and revitalized. The site was named the Wrigley Memorial and Botanical Garden and is currently operated by the Catalina Island Conservancy.

El Rancho Escondido, Wrigley's Arabian horse ranch, was established in Catalina Island's interior in 1932. Wrigley believed the island's interior had infinite potential and wanted to make it more accessible to the island's visitors. Much of his father's efforts were spent in Avalon building the resort amenities, and Philip believed that if he could draw attention to the island's interior, it would open up a new world for visitors to explore. He built El Rancho Escondido (the Hidden Ranch) as a retreat for his family and as a symbol that the interior did in fact exist.

The ranch continued to grow during the 1930s as Wrigley had planned. He wanted a self-sufficient, working ranch that would be accessible to visitors. By the time his ranch was ready, the military stepped in at the onset of World War II and closed the island to tourism. Wrigley's dream of opening up Catalina's interior would have to wait. After the war, the Santa Catalina Island Company started the Inland Motor Tour that tours the island's interior and stops at El Rancho Escondido. Since that time, thousands of visitors have enjoyed the island's interior views and Wrigley's Arabian horse ranch.

By the early 1940s, Catalina's brochures boasted "Everything for Your Enjoyment" and it was true! The island had grown into the ideal resort community. Visitors enjoyed a range of accommodations and amenities and participated in many exciting activities, such as golf, fishing, stagecoach rides, boat tours, interior tours, swimming, dancing, shopping, and much more.

Horseback riding was a popular activity and a great way to see the island. Horse stables have been located in Avalon Canyon for more than 100 years.

Tour buses were introduced to the Santa Catalina Island Company's fleet in the early 1950s. The open coach-style buses were used for the Avalon Scenic Drive and the island's interior tours.

Once aquaplaning was introduced to visitors in the 1920s, it became a Catalina favorite. Aquaplanes were wide wooden boards that were pulled behind a speedboat, similar to water skiing or wave boarding. Aquaplane races across the channel were an annual event for many years.

Each summer Avalon's harbor would fill with yachts and sailboats, the steamers made daily trips, and glassbottom boats took passengers back and forth to the marine gardens. The harbor could sometimes be just as busy as the City of Avalon. Avalon's harbormaster and patrolmen have long maintained the harbor as a safe destination for all boaters.

Entertainment in the casino building continued to flourish during Wrigley's tenure. The building hosted such legends as the Buddy Rogers Orchestra (pictured), Dick Jurgens, Kay Kyser, and Jimmy Dorsey.

Many of the big bands serenaded the visitors and residents of Avalon from the terrace balcony of the casino building. Bands were also known to play a Spanish lullaby as the steamer sailed out of Avalon Bay for its return to the mainland.

DANCE YOUR CARES AWAY

WITH THE *Melody Master*

Listen in every night at 9:30 and 11:00 over KHJ and the Don Lee Network

Hal GRAYSON AND HIS ORCHESTRA

NOW AT THE SANTA CATALINA ISLAND *Casino*

EVERY NIGHT AND SUNDAY AFTERNOONS

WTCo 33

One of Wrigley's major contributions to the island and its music was to broadcast the casino's bands across the nation's airwaves. In 1934, Wrigley, along with his close friend Les Atlas of the Columbia Broadcasting Company, arranged for nightly broadcasts of big band music from the casino ballroom. The broadcasts continued with few interruptions through the 1950s. During this time, listeners from across the nation heard, "From the beautiful casino ballroom, overlooking Avalon Bay at Catalina Island, we bring you the music of . . ." The magical sounds of the era's most notable big bands introduced America to the casino ballroom and Catalina Island.

Speaking of notable, the Jimmy Dorsey Orchestra was a favorite during the 1951 summer season. Dorsey was joined that season by the Woody Herman, Stan Kenton, and the Ray Whitaker Orchestras.

In 1931, the Santa Catalina Island Company, under the direction of Wrigley, started the Wilmington-Catalina Airline and opened Hamilton Beach Airport. The small airport was built in Hamilton Cove and had a unique turntable system for turning the seaplanes in tight quarters. The terminal building of the airport was built in the Spanish Colonial style and included a ticket office, a Catalina tile–lined waiting room, a refreshment counter, and a lovely garden waiting area. Wilmington-Catalina Airlines operated Loening Amphibians and Douglas Dolphins.

Wilmington-Catalina Airline's Douglas Dolphins were specially designed for use on Catalina Island by Donald Douglas. Douglas was a frequent visitor to Catalina Island and a friend to Wrigley. The hull of the Dolphin was designed after a boat hull to cut the water sharply. Two engines placed above the wing powered these seaplanes that could carry up to ten passengers. Wilmington-Catalina Airlines operated five Douglas Dolphins.

The Grumman G-21 Goose was developed in 1936. Originally intended for use as a private executive seaplane, the rugged amphibians were used extensively in World War II. Grumman Goose Amphibians were first used to carry passengers to Santa Catalina Island in 1948, and they were a perfect fit. For four decades the planes were flown by numerous airlines, carrying both passengers and freight.

In 1957 a Sikorsky VS-44A flying boat was put into passenger service on Catalina Island by Avalon Air Transport. Avalon Air Transport began seaplane operations on Catalina in 1953 and claims the longest continuous service to the island. Their Sikorsky VS-44A, affectionately known as the "Mother Goose," had a wingspan of 124 feet and was originally designed to carry 20 passengers by day and to accommodate 16 berths at night. For Catalina service, the plane's interior was modified to carry 47 passengers and a crew of 4. The "Mother Goose" flew between Avalon and Long Beach Harbor until she was retired and sold in 1967. Today, Catalina's "Mother Goose" can be found at the New England Air Museum in Windsor Locks, Connecticut.

Always interested in aviation, Wrigley wanted to build an airport in the island's interior for easier access to his Arabian horse ranch. After years of study to yield a building site, construction of the Airport-in-the-Sky commenced in August of 1940. Two mountain tops had to be leveled and the valleys between filled to provide a flat surface for the runway. This large task took several months and was finished just in time for the military to declare the airport inoperable during World War II. After the war, airport buildings were completed, the runway was surfaced, and the Airport-in-the-Sky opened in 1946.

United Airlines was the first carrier to service Catalina Island with DC-3s out of the Airport-in-the-Sky. Wilmington-Catalina Airlines changed their company name to Catalina Airlines and moved their operations to the interior airport, and several other island seaplane operations began using the Airport-in-the-Sky for landings during bad weather. The airport is now open for private plane use and is a popular destination for pilots in Southern California.

The Chicago Cubs continued their training on Catalina Island under the direction of Wrigley after his father's death in 1932. The Cubs spent several weeks on the island each spring, training and enjoying the island. This team photograph of the 1932 National League Championship team was taken in 1933. Note the Catalina Country Club in the background, which served as the team's clubhouse during its stay.

Wrigley enjoyed the Chicago Cubs players and would host barbecues for the team at his ranch in the island's interior. Wrigley also organized an exhibition match on the island between the Chicago Cubs and the New York Giants in memory of his father. The most significant contribution Wrigley made to the world of baseball was the development of the National Women's Baseball League during World War II.

During the 1950s, Catalina Island was host to a great motorcycle race series known as the Catalina Grand Prix. Several Southern California sportsmen approached Wrigley with the idea, and through the combined efforts of the Santa Catalina Island Company and countless individuals, clubs, and dealers, a race was born. The race was strictly for sport, no cash price was ever rewarded, nor was there an admission fee.

For seven years during the 1950s, each May more than 300 motorcycles and thousands of spectators would descend upon Avalon for the Catalina Grand Prix. The riders faced ten laps on a four and a half mile course that led riders over city streets, winding paths, onto dirt roads, and along a horse trail. Over the years, many skilled riders crossed the finish line into Catalina Island history.

The Diving Bell was built in 1950 on Casino Point to offer visitors a thrilling way to see Catalina's beautiful underwater environment. The bell had several glass ports around the walls to view sea life and enough room for 12 people. The steel bell weighed three tons and entered and exited the water on a central guide shaft by a motor driven cable. The ascent and descent were generally slow, but many recall the real excitement occurred when the cable was released and the buoyant bell would shoot to the surface like a cork. The Diving Bell thrilled visitors on Casino Point for 11 years.

During the late 1940s and 1950s, Wrigley did much to promote and advertise Catalina Island to the world. Wrigley had previously worked with advertising artists Otis and Dorothy Shepard to create an early California look for Avalon that he considered the foundation for promoting Catalina. Wrigley employed a publicist and hired photographers to capture life and events on the island. This fabulous photograph is one of the many publicity shots used by the Santa Catalina Island Company.

Catalina's charm continued to lure celebrities throughout the 1930s. Mickey Rooney and Johnny Weismuller, pictured here at Catalina's Golf Links, were both frequent Catalina visitors. Rooney also filmed several movies on the island, including *You're Only Young Once*, an Andy Hardy movie about a family trip to Catalina Island. The SS *Avalon, Miss Catalina* speedboats, and the casino ballroom were all featured in this film.

Wrigley and his wife, Helen, enjoy a beautiful day on the Catalina Golf Links with Stan Laurel, Oliver Hardy, and their wives. Laurel and Hardy were also frequent visitors to Catalina Island in the 1930s.

Humphrey Bogart takes a stroll on the beach at Catalina's isthmus with a friend.

John Wayne was a favorite among Catalina's local residents. Wayne would sail his yacht to the island with his wife, and they would stroll along Catalina's streets, shop, visit with their island friends, and frequent the local eateries. Wayne is pictured here with Duke Fishman, a Catalina celebrity in his own right. Duke Fishman was a lifeguard on Catalina Island for many years and would entertain visitors during the steamer greetings each afternoon. He was also an actor and worked as an extra on many of the movies that were filmed on the island. Duke was a true Catalina character!

Catalina's isthmus is so-called because it has two coves separated by approximately a half mile of land. When Spanish explorers first discovered the island, they assumed there were two islands, but there is only one Catalina Island. This photograph shows Isthmus Cove in the 1920s. At this time, the isthmus was primarily used for motion picture production, which might explain the castle-like structure near the pier.

Originally called Union Harbor by the soldiers who were stationed at the isthmus during the Civil War, Isthmus Cove was developed as a yachting destination in the 1920s. The town was named Two Harbors and local yachtsmen soon claimed the isthmus and its surrounding coves as their summer retreat.

By 1940 Catalina Island was in its heyday. Tourism had increased steadily throughout the 1930s as Catalina gained the reputation as an enchanting resort community. Many of the improvements and construction projects initiated by William and Philip Wrigley were complete, and the island was in its full glory. Everything was going swimmingly for Avalon until the island and country were stunned by the attack on Pearl Harbor.

The initial effects of World War II on Catalina Island were seen in transportation, which was and still is the island's lifeblood. Within two weeks of the invasion at Pearl Harbor, the United States Coast Guard ordered regularly scheduled steamship passenger service ceased. Catalina Island was declared a federal military zone and the San Pedro Channel was designated a controlled area for vessels. The cessation of steamer service to the island meant no tourists, and as the summer season approached, it became clear that the island's resort activities would be shut down. Within a year, the island was so deserted that the Santa Catalina Island Company began to actively pursue various branches of the military to use the island towards the war effort.

The United States Maritime Service answered the Santa Catalina Island Company's call to use the island. They set up an extensive training station in Avalon in 1942. The United States Maritime Service leased the Hotel Atwater, Hotel St. Catherine, Island Villas, Chicago Cubs ballpark and clubhouse, the hospital, Catalina Island Yacht Club, and the casino building. Many homes and apartments in town were rented to station personnel and military families as well. Maritime Service trainees are pictured here on the Chicago Cubs ballpark.

United States Maritime Service recruits were sent to the training station on Catalina Island for two to four months to receive a variety of training. The Maritime Service was a branch of the United States War Shipping Administration and under the jurisdiction of the United States Navy. The Maritime Service was established to train personnel for merchant ships. The trainees received extensive physical training and were expected to master several skills including how to abandon ship, swim through oil and fire, man lifeboats, and fire anti-air craft guns. Trainees are pictured here conducting a flaming water drill.

Anti-aircraft guns exactly like the ones found on United States Navy merchant ships were mounted on Casino Point, and Maritime Service recruits were expected to master their firing. The Maritime Service also had four training ships at Avalon and built sections of ships on land for further training.

Along with the anti-aircraft guns, two wooden buildings were constructed on Casino Point. After the completion of a 13-week boot camp, the servicemen were given a variety of tests to determine in what job they would be placed. The Avalon Training Station produced thousands of deckhands, oilers, firemen, water tenders, cooks, and bakers who made significant contributions to the war effort.

In November 1942, the United States Coast Guard declared the entire isthmus area of the island a highly restricted military reservation, and vigilant around-the-clock sentry posts were established in strategic locations. No vessels were permitted to anchor or moor in Isthmus Cove or Catalina Harbor, and many private yachts were requisitioned by the Coast Guard to be used for patrol. The Coast Guard set up a sophisticated training station at the isthmus where new recruits received two months of extensive training in all phases of seagoing skills.

United States Coast Guard trainees received training in basic seamanship, small boat handling, close order drill, manual of arms, gunnery, first aid, chemical war defense, fire fighting, operating whale boats, live weapon firing, and sentry duties, to name a few. This photograph shows recruits undergoing live gas mask training at the isthmus in 1943.

The United States Army Signal Corps set up a sophisticated radar station on Catalina Island in 1942. Camp Cactus was established in Catalina's interior to monitor enemy activity. The Signal Corps's radar station and several strategically placed bunkers were linked directly to Fort Mac Arthur, Los Angeles's main line of coastal defense during the war.

The mission of Camp Cactus was to detect the approach of Japanese warplanes or ships. This was accomplished with the installation of radio transmitters and antennas. This secret radar system was quite advanced for the time and, once operational, could detect enemy activity from miles away. This camp extended Ft. McArthur's defense perimeter far beyond the coast. The site was protected by infantry, anti-aircraft, and artillery. This photograph shows stationed military personnel outside their barracks at Camp Cactus in 1943.

The Office of Strategic Services, now known as the Central Intelligence Agency, set up a small training station on Catalina Island at Toyon Bay in 1943. The base was top secret; most island residents did not realize the OSS was on the island during the war. Men were trained at the Toyon facility to become experts with weapons and explosives. They were trained in martial arts and covert operations as well as survival training, hand-to-hand combat, map reading, cryptography, and radio operations. Many of the men were later sent to Burma and China where they did behind-the-lines intelligence work. This photograph shows one OSS training class that included many Americans of Japanese and Hawaiian descent.

In Memoriam

November, 1944

U.S.NAVY

| THOMAS H. RALSTON | WALLIS H. MARRIAGE | GORDON F. KAISER |
| THOMAS R. SMITH | EDWARD T. GORSKI | PRESTON L. GIRARD |

The United States Navy's *King III* airship was conducting a training mission when it lost its course and crashed into a hillside in Upper Avalon Canyon on October 17, 1944. The airship had departed Del Mar, California to conduct a 22-hour night navigation training operation. When the ship was near the island, the weather began to limit its visibility and the airship hit a hillside on the island carrying 700 gallons of fuel. The explosion instantly killed five of the nine-man crew, and another crew member died of his injuries in the following days. These airships were employed by the United States Navy for antisubmarine patrol during the war.

At the end of World War II, the military packed up and left Catalina Island. The island's steamships, which had been previously requisitioned by the government, were returned and life slowly went back to normal. By the following summer season, the island was ready to

welcome tourists again. The summer of 1946 was Catalina's triumphant return as a resort destination and hosted thousands of visitors who danced to the big band sounds of Jimmy Grier and Leighton Noble.

The long-standing steamer pier was dismantled in the late 1960s and the Cabrillo Mole was built. The mole was part of an overall plan for harbor improvement by the City of Avalon and was designed as a docking facility for several ships. The Cabrillo Mole was finished in time for the 1969 season and has since served as Avalon's primary dock.

The Santa Catalina Island Company continued under Wrigley's direction until his death in 1977. He made many significant contributions to the island, but none more important than the organization of the Catalina Island Conservancy. Wrigley had been exploring uses for the island's interior for many years and wanted to ensure its preservation as open space. Establishing the Catalina Island Conservancy was the best option. In 1974, Wrigley transferred 42,135 acres of Catalina Island to the recently established Catalina Island Conservancy. The conservancy is a nonprofit organization dedicated to the preservation of Catalina Island's native plants, animals and environments. The conservancy's land is open to the public for hiking and camping year round. This one act by Wrigley ensured that the unspoiled beauty of Catalina Island will remain for future generations to enjoy. (Courtesy of Santa Catalina Island Company Collection.)

126

Philip Wrigley's son William took over the reigns of the Santa Catalina Island Company and the William Wrigley Jr. Company after his father's death in 1977. William was already intimately involved with the family's interests, having been the executive officer of the William Wrigley Jr. Company since 1961. He spent much time on the island during his childhood with his parents and sisters and would bring his own family to the island as an adult. Wrigley carried on his grandfather's dream and the family interests until his death in 1999.

William Wrigley Jr. is the son of William, grandson of Philip and great grandson of his namesake William Wrigley Jr. He is the chief executive officer of the William Wrigley Jr. Company in Chicago where his business keeps him most of the time. However, he does keep a sharp eye on the family's Catalina interests with the help of his sister Alison Wrigley Rusack, who sits on the board of trustees of the Catalina Island Conservancy, and his cousin Paxson Offield, chairman of the board and chief executive officer of the Santa Catalina Island Company.

For almost 100 years, Catalina Island was in the hands of visionary businessmen who believed in her limitless potential. These men, with the aid of countless others, built a world-renowned resort community and ensured the preservation of the island's open spaces for generations to come.

Much has changed over the years, but the lure of Catalina Island remains the same—an enchanting island out in the blue Pacific for your enjoyment!